W9-AJO-562

RUNNING FOR PUBLIC OFFICE

A **TRUE** BOOK

by

Sarah De Capua

Children's Press®

A Division of Scholastic Inc.

New York Toronto London Auckland Sydney
Mexico City New Delhi Hong Kong
Danbury, Connecticut

A candidate for Congress on the campaign trail

Reading Consultant
Nanci R. Vargus, Ed.D.
Teacher in Residence
University of Indianapolis
Indianapolis, Indiana

The photograph on the cover shows a candidate for city council campaigning during a parade. The photograph on the title page shows Dianne Feinstein of California giving a victory speech during her campaign for the U.S. Senate in 1992.

Library of Congress Cataloging-in-Publication Data

De Capua, Sarah.
    Running for public office / by Sarah De Capua.
        p. cm. — (A True book)
    Includes bibliographical references and index.
    Summary: Describes the process of running for a public office, including the planning and organizing of a campaign, the campaign trail, and election day.
    ISBN 0-516-22333-X (lib. bdg.)   0-516-27368-X (pbk.)
    1. Political campaigns—United States—Juvenile literature. 2. Campaign management—United States—Juvenile literature. 3. Politics, Practical—United States—Juvenile literature. [1. Politics, Practical. 2. Elections.] I. Title. II. Series.
JK2281.D4 2002
324.7'0973—dc21   2001007944

© 2002 by Children's Press
A Division of Scholastic Inc.
All rights reserved. Published simultaneously in Canada.
Printed in the United States of America.

CHILDREN'S PRESS, AND A TRUE BOOK®, and associated logos are trademarks and or registered trademarks of Grolier Publishing Co., Inc. SCHOLASTIC and associated logos are trademarks and or registered trademarks of Scholastic Inc.

1 2 3 4 5 6 7 8 9 10 R 11 10 09 08 07 06 05 04 03 02

Contents

Governors, such as Gary Locke of Washington State, are public officeholders.

What Is a Public Office?

Do you ever hear adults say, "If I were the mayor, I would . . ." or, "If I were the president . . ."? Mayors and the president of the United States are people who hold public office. A state's governor, senators, and representatives are public officeholders too. Other public officeholders

The presidency is the highest public office in the United States.

include members of a town council or school board.

A public officeholder is someone who has been elected or appointed to a government job. People in public office serve the members of a community. Public officeholders may work for the government of a town, city, county, state, or nation.

Different public officeholders have different roles and responsibilities. For example, mayors, governors, and the president of the United States are the heads of their governments. City-council members and members of the

A city-council meeting in North Carolina

U.S. Congress create laws. School-board members make sure their community's schools are run well.

The United States is a democracy. In a democracy, people choose their leaders through elections. During an election, people vote for candidates they believe will do the best job in various public offices.

Voters should learn as much as they can about candidates. They must know where candidates

Voters usually support candidates whose views on important issues are similar to their own.

stand on issues that voters care about. These issues might include such things as taxes, education, the environment, or civil rights.

9

Public officeholders, such as the mayor of New York City, have the opportunity to help their communities.

Public officeholders have the opportunity to help their community. This is why most people decide to try to become public officeholders. But being in public office is not an easy job. It requires a lot of hard work and dedication.

Before a person can hold a public office, he or she usually must win the position. The candidate must convince voters that he or she will do a better job than anyone else. This is

People running for public office must convince voters that they are the best person for the job.

called running for public office. It is also known as a campaign.

Running for public office is a full-time job. It takes a

It takes a lot of time and effort for a candidate to run for public office.

lot of time and effort. In the following chapters, you will learn about some of the steps people take to run for public office.

Political Parties

A political party is an organized group of people with similar beliefs about how the government should be run. Usually, people running for public office belong to a party. This helps give voters a general idea of where the candidate stands on important issues.

The two largest political parties in the United States are the Democratic Party and the Republican Party. Democrats believe in a strong central government whose policies favor social change. Republicans believe in a limited role of the central government and more individual responsibility.

A Republican supporter at a political rally

Volunteers sending out mailings supporting local Democratic candidates

Planning and Organizing a Campaign

A person who wants to run for office must first decide how he or she can best serve the public. It is important to answer the following questions:

- What issues are important to the people I will be serving?

- What are my views on those issues?

15

A congressman announcing his candidacy for the U.S. Senate

- How could I do the job better than the person who holds the office now?

- Why do I want this job?

- How much time can I give to my campaign?

- How much time can I give to the job?

A candidate talking to voters about issues

People thinking about running for public office usually get advice from their family and friends to help them make their decision.

Once a person has decided to run for public office, the

A candidate for U.S. Congress planning her campaign

planning and organizing begin. A campaign for a local office, such as mayor, may last only a few months. Other campaigns, such as presidential campaigns, begin more than a year before the election.

First, a candidate must go to the local elections office or clerk's office to obtain a petition form for the desired public office. The petition lists the candidate's name and address and the office he or she is seeking. The candidate must get a certain number of registered voters to sign the petition to show they support him or her. The candidate then files the petition at the elections or clerk's office. Every state, county, town, or village may have different requirements and forms to fill out in order to run for public office.

Candidates must raise money to pay for their campaign. Some candidates use their own money. Most ask supporters to contribute money.

Running for public office costs a lot of money. Candidates need money to pay for their headquarters, phone bills, and electricity bills. Money is also needed for printing brochures and letters

The campaign headquarters of a candidate for the U.S Congress

about the candidate, and for postage to mail that information to voters. Money is needed to buy computers and office supplies, as well as to buy advertising on radio, television, and in newspapers.

One way candidates raise money is by keeping a list of voters. This list is usually kept on a computer. It contains the names and addresses of every person who is eligible to vote for that candidate. Candidates ask for money from the voters who are most likely to vote for them. This money is called a contribution (kon-trib-YOO-shun).

Another important part of planning and organizing a campaign is finding people to

Members of the campaign staff of
Republican presidential candidate
George W. Bush during the 2000 election

work for the candidate.
Candidates usually hire someone to be in charge of their
campaign. This person is
called a campaign manager.
Most campaign managers are

paid to work for the candidate. Many other people are asked to be volunteers. A volunteer is a person who does a job without being paid.

Volunteers are an important part of any campaign. They help the candidate get his or her message out to the voters. Volunteers put out signs with the candidate's name. They work at campaign headquarters. There they stuff and address envelopes full of

Volunteers for various candidates handing out materials (top), putting out signs (bottom left), and preparing a mailing (bottom right)

A candidate (center) meeting
voters at a volunteer's home

information about the candidate. Volunteers then mail
the envelopes to voters.

Some volunteers host
gatherings in their home so

neighbors can meet the candidate. Other volunteers walk through neighborhoods going door-to-door to talk to voters about the candidate. Volunteers also contact voters by telephone to ask for contributions or to ask people to vote for their candidate.

Once a candidate has organized all of the people, money, and materials needed for the campaign, there is still plenty of work to be done.

You Can Help Too!

Adults are not the only people who can volunteer in a campaign. A lot of kids your age can get involved too. Learn about the views of different candidates and volunteer for one whose ideas you like. You can stuff envelopes, make signs, and help keep the candidate's headquarters clean and organized. It's a great way to learn about running for public office. And it could be a good experience for you—especially if you ever decide to run for public office yourself!

On the Campaign Trail

When the campaign has begun, the candidate must focus on getting as many people as possible to vote for him or her. There are many methods candidates use to get votes.

Candidate Pete Wilson campaigning for governor of California (top), and a political rally for Democratic presidential candidate Al Gore in 2000 (bottom)

Some of these include:

• **Rallies**—A rally is a large meeting. Rallies are usually held outside or in large enclosed places. At a political rally, voters gather in support of a particular candidate. The candidate attends the rally and makes a speech.

• **Walking door-to-door**—This method is most often used by candidates running for local office. A candidate walks door-to-door to meet people and ask for their vote. It is almost

A candidate (left)
campaigning door-to-door

impossible for candidates in state
or national campaigns to use this
method. There would be too
many homes to visit!

• **Campaign signs**—Signs help
make the candidate's name
known to voters. Volunteers offer

supporters signs for their lawns or bumper stickers for their cars. Signs also appear along roadsides and in the windows of some businesses. Large outdoor signs, called bill-boards, may be put up along highways or freeways.

Supporters holding campaign signs on Election Day

A television ad for a candidate

- **Radio and television commercials**—Commercials help voters find out how the candidate plans to help the community and solve problems. Candidates running for state or national office are more likely to use commercials than those who are running for local office. Some candidates place advertisements in newspapers as well.

• **Web sites**—Candidates set up Web sites that contain information about the candidate's personal life, how he or she can best serve the people, and position on various issues. Many sites contain the candidate's E-mail address. Voters can E-mail questions to the candidate.

Senator Bill Bradley answers voters' questions while campaigning for president in 1999.

Not every candidate uses every method. Some methods work better than others. But all of these methods are aimed at getting voters to like a candidate. If voters like a candidate, they will vote for him or her!

Election Day

A candidate may have worked for many weeks or months on his or her campaign. All of the work has been in preparation for one day—Election Day. Election Day is the day set aside for eligible voters to cast their vote for a particular candidate. However, even when Election

A candidate (right) greeting a voter on Election Day

Day arrives, the candidate's work continues.

In a local election, candidates may visit polling places. They greet voters in one final attempt to get their vote. Candidates in state or national elections may make appearances in specific cities or states where they feel they need more votes.

On the night of the election, candidates often host parties or gatherings while they wait for the results to come in. The parties are usually held in hotel ballrooms or school gymnasiums. The candidates and their families, as well as the volunteers who worked on their campaigns,

An election-night gathering for a Los Angeles mayoral candidate (center)

George W. Bush (left) watching election returns with his parents during the 2000 presidential election

attend the parties. Many of the candidate's supporters are also invited to attend.

Each candidate hosts his or her own party. Later in the evening, the results of the voting become known. The candidate who wins gives a victory speech. He or she thanks the voters and

The winner of a state senate seat in Wisconsin gives her victory speech

the people who worked on the campaign. The winner speaks about the ways he or she will help the people as their elected official.

The candidate who loses the election gives a concession (kuhn-SESH-uhn) speech. The partygoers are disappointed

A candidate for governor
of New Jersey giving a
concession speech

that their candidate lost. The
candidate is disappointed too.
But it is important to be a
good sport about losing. The
candidate thanks his or her
supporters and the people
who worked on the campaign.

He or she wishes the winner success as the elected official.

Running for public office is a hard job. Winning the election is a great reward. But getting elected is not the end. The truly hard work of serving the public has just begun!

New York Governor George Pataki signing a bill into law

To Find Out More

Here are some additional resources to help you learn more about running for public office:

 **Books**

Brooks, Walter R. **Freddy the Politician.** Overlook Press, 2000.

De Capua, Sarah. **Voting.** Children's Press, 2002.

Sobel, Syl. **Presidential Elections and Other Cool Facts.** Barrons Juveniles, 2000.

Organizations and Online Sites

County Clerk or State Board of Elections

Look in your local telephone book for the county clerk's or state board of elections office in your area. There you will find a lot of information about the rules for organizing a campaign in your town and how volunteers can get involved.

Federal Election Commission

999 E Street NW
Washington, DC 20463
http://www.fec.gov

This site contains a link where citizens can learn about campaigns for federal office, rules and regulations for running for federal office, and elections and voting in general.

Running for Office

http://www.uky.edu/LCC/HIS/271/running.html

This site explains in detail the steps involved in running for public office.

Running Political Campaigns

http://usinfo.state.gov/usa/infousa/politics/govworks

This site is dedicated to the way candidates run and manage political campaigns. Includes links to related sites.

45

Important Words

appointed chosen rather than elected for a public office

brochure booklet, usually with pictures, that contains information

community the people living in a particular place

council group of people that makes decisions

county part of a state with its own local government

eligible satisfying all requirements

issues problems that need to be solved

polling place building, such as a school or library, where voters cast their votes

supporters people who plan to vote for a certain candidate

Index

Meet the Author

Sarah De Capua received her master of arts in teaching degree in 1993 and has since been educating children, first as a teacher and currently as an editor and author of children's books. Other books she has written for Children's Press include *Becoming a Citizen, Paying Taxes, Serving on a Jury,* and *Voting* (True Books); *J.C. Watts, Jr.: Character Counts* (Community Builders); and several titles in the Rookie Read-About® Geography series.

Ms. De Capua resides in Colorado.

Photographs © 2002: AP/Wide World Photos: 4 (Louie Balukoff), 23 (Harry Cabluck), 40 (Eric Draper), 41 (Liana J. Griffith/Journal Times), 42 (Daniel Hulshizer); Archive Photos/Getty Images/Reuters: 28 center; Corbis Sygma/Chris Usher: 30 bottom; Corbis-Bettmann: 13 (AFP), 16 (Reuters NewMedia Inc.); Getty Images: 39 (David McNew/Newsmakers), 6 (Rick Wilking/Newsmakers); Jim West: 9; Jim Whitmer Photography: 14 top; Photo Researchers, NY/Doug Martin: 34; PhotoEdit: 14 bottom (Paul Conklin), 28 bottom (Michael Newman), 18, 21 (Jonathan Nourok), 32 (Mark Richards); Photri Inc./Bachmann: 26; Richard B. Levine: 2, 10; Stock Boston: 25 top (Chromosohm/Sohm), cover, 17, 25 bottom right, 28 top (Bob Daemmrich), 36 (Najlah Feanny), 7 (Charles Gupton), 30 top (A. Ramey), 25 bottom left (Rhoda Sidney), 33 (Peter Southwick), 1 (Gary Wagner); The Image Works: 12 (Bob Daemmrich), 43 (David M. Jennings), 38 (Larry Kolvoord)